Vegan Foodi Multi Cooker Cookbook

Over 500 Quick, Easy and Delicious 100% Vegan Recipes on Foodi Pressure Cooker with Zero Meat Recipes

Melissa Richmond

Copyright © 2020 by Melissa Richmond

Table of Contents

Introduction

Congratulations for purchasing a copy of this book Vegan Foodi Multi Cooker Cookbook Featuring over 500 Quick, Easy and Delicious 100% Vegan Recipes on Foodi Pressure Cooker with Zero Bacon and Meat recipes.

One of the major challenges most of us face is the time to prepare food due to our very busy schedules

Why spend a fortune and buy a ton of different kitchen appliances when you could do with just one? Have you ever imagined the leisure of having your pressure cooker, slow cooker, Air fryer, Sauté pan and Rice cooker all in one?

The Foodi Pressure Cooker turns this imagination into reality. It's easy to use, saves you load of time, and cleanup is a breeze.

The Foodi Multi-cooker is revolutionary! You can cook virtually anything in a Multi-cooker – from meats and main courses to rice, potatoes, vegetables of every description, dessert to even yogurt. Better yet, pressure cooking and air frying cooking allows you to prepare foods up to 70% faster than conventional cooking methods do, which means you save energy in addition to your time!

What is especially great is that you can use the Foodi to create tons of Vegan dishes too. Machines that will help you reach your diet goals? Sounds like something you should get right now!

Veganism, however, is much more than a diet. It is a way of life. Those who choose a vegan lifestyle not only eat plant-based foods but also choose not to purchase products made from leather, wool, and silk and down, including cosmetics and soaps that contain animal products or are tested on animals. So vegan is a lifestyle and for you to purchase this book, it shows how you are serious with your vegan diet.

As a vegan, preparing your dishes with Foodi Cooker is another way of getting your diet prepared quickly and deliciously.

This book gives a detailed explanation on how to make use of your Foodi Multi-Cooker device, every information you need to know about Vegan Diet with over 500 Quick, Easy and Delicious 100% Vegan Recipes on Foodi Pressure Cooker with Zero Meat recipes.

Chapter One: Vegan A Lifestyle

Veganism is not just another newfangled diet or passing fad. Plant-based and animal product-free diets have been around for centuries. Even the terms "vegan" has been in circulation for decades. In the 1940s, several members of England's then nearly one-hundred-year-old Vegetarian society spilt off to form their own organization that focused on a strictly plant-based diet that eschewed all animal-derived foods. These strict vegetarians chose the name "vegan" because, as one of the founding members of the first Vegan Society, Donald Watson, said, "Veganism start with vegetarianism and carries it through to its logical conclusion"

A vegan diet can be defined as a "total vegetarian" diet, meaning one that is entirely plant-based and omits all animal products, including meats, eggs, dairy, honey, gelatin, and other products that comes from animals. Vegans eat a plant-based diet of vegetables, grains, legumes, fruits, nuts and seeds.

Veganism, however, is much more than a diet. It is a way of life. Those who choose a vegan lifestyle not only eat plant-based foods but also choose not to purchase products made from leather, wool, and silk and down, including cosmetics and soaps that contain animal products or are tested on animals.

Types of vegans

Guidelines and Rules for Eating Vegan

A vegan diet can be a very healthy way of eating, as long as it's well balanced to ensure that you are getting the right mix of nutrients. Since veganism eliminates all animal-derived foods, it can be a bit of a challenge to meet your daily needs for certain nutrients that are primarily found in animal products, such as vitamin B12, vitamin D, calcium, iron, iodine, omega-3 fatty acids, zinc, and even protein.

Eat Your Veggies and Fruits

Every good diet starts with eating the recommended five or more servings of fruits and vegetables each day. This ensures that you get a wide range of vitamins, minerals, and antioxidants. These are the ingredients of a healthy et d the nutrients that decrease your risk of disease like heart disease, stroke, and many types of cancer, of-course, if your diet is solely plant-based, this part is a piece of cake

Calcium

Calcium, which is crucial for building and maintaining strong bones and healthy muscles and nerves, is most commonly derived from animal products such as milk and other dairy products, but dark and leafy green vegetables-think kale, chard, collard greens, and broccoli-can provide sufficient quantities of calcium if you eat enough of them You can also buy calcium-fortified juices, breads, cereals, soy milk, and other products to make sure you are getting enough. Most adults should consume 1000 to 1200 milligrams per day of calcium, either through foods sources or as supplements.

Iodine

Iodine is another important nutrient that keeps your thyroid running smoothly. While many food sources of iodine are animal-based (dairy products, eggs, and fish) High concentrations can also be found in sea vegetables and strawberries. Iodized salt is fortified with iodine. Most adults need about 150 micrograms of iodine per day.

Iron

Iron is essential for developing red blood cells. Iron from meat is the mostly easily absorbed by the human body, but there are many plant-based sources of iron as well. Dried beans, iron-fortified cereals and breads, whole-grain foods, dark and leafy green vegetables, and dried fruit all contain ample amounts of iron. To maximize your absorption of the iron in their foods combine them with rich sources of vitamins C, such as strawberries, citrus fruits, tomatoes, cabbage, and broccoli

Omega-3 Fatty Acids

Omega-3 fatty acids help regulate metabolism and reduce the risk of cardiovascular disease. The most common dietary sources of these essential fatty acids are fish and eggs, but they can be found in canola oil or soy oil, walnuts, flaxseed, and soybeans.

Vitamin B12

Vitamins B12 are vitally important because it plays a key role in cell metabolism, the normal functioning of the brain and nervous system, and the formation of blood. It's found naturally in animal-based foods, including meat, fish, poultry, eggs, and dairy products, but many vegan-friendly foods are fortified with a synthetic form of vitamin B12, including soy milk and breakfast cereals. Supplements are also available in the form of pills, sublingual's, or injections. Aim to eat at least 3 micrograms per day in fortified foods or take a 10-microgram supplement daily.

Vitamin D

Like calcium, vitamin D is important for maintaining healthy bones. Many nondairy milks, however, are also fortified with vitamin D, as are many cereals and breads. Most adults need a minimum of 200 to 400 international units of vitamin D each day.

Zinc

Zinc plays a critical role in keeping the immune system strong as well as in cell division and formation of proteins. Like iron, zinc from plant sources is not absorbed by the body as easily as that from animal products such as diary. Good vegan sources of zinc include soybeans and products made with soybeans (such as tofu), whole grains, legumes, nuts and wheat germ.

Equipment required to Prepare Your Vegan Dishes

Equipping your kitchen Going vegan means mindful eating so you wil most likely give up on most processed foods. You will probably cook fo yourself and require certain kitchen utensils to make the transition smoother.

Here is a list:

- Food processor, small blender, blender, and/or immersion blender

- Measuring tools, i.e., measuring spoons, dry and liqui measuring cups

- Veggie peeler, potato masher, grater, spiralizer, and othe similar tools.

- Bamboo steamer, mesh strainer, colander

- Mortar and pestle

- Tea kettle

- Whisk, tongs, ladle, wooden spoons, silicon brush, good knive: spatulas

- Cutting board(s)

- Wok, pots, frying pans, sheet pans, oven-proof pans, an assorted lids.

- Mason jars, mixing bowls, salad bowls

As you start cooking and develop a taste for vegan foods, you wi discover the exact utensils that you will need. Some need a foc processor daily, some don't. It really depends on what you want to cook. Some need a julienned tool; others prefer to use a knife. Some use a blender for guacamole, others use a mortar and pestle. Most kitchen utensils are common, and people already have them in their kitchens. It really depends on how much you used to cook before going vegan.

Vegan Kitchen

A vegan's pantry must be well-stocked. Here are the ingredients you should make sure you always have:

Vegan essentials: miso, tofu, tempeh, nutritional yeast, tahini, nori sheets, kelp, kombu, hijiki, coconut milk, coconut cream, plant-based milks, soy sauce, protein powder, seitan, agar-agar, nut butters, vegan-friendly vitamins (especially B12)

Essential fruits and veggies: frozen fruits, frozen veggies, lemons, bananas, cashews, greens, sweet potatoes, mushrooms, berries, avocados, bell peppers

"Meat" replacements: veggie broth, vegan mayo, vegan cheeses, vegan yogurts, agar-agar (vegan gelatin), vegan chocolate (dark chocolate)

Canned beans: lentils, chickpeas, pinto, black, kidney, and cannellini beans, edamame, peas

Grains: Brown, wild, and white rice, quinoa, farro, spelt, bulgur, millet, oats

Flours: almond flour, coconut flour, wholegrain flours, plain flour, etc.

Seeds: chia seeds, flax seeds, cumin seeds, sesame seeds, pumpkin seeds, sunflower seeds, etc.

Nuts: walnuts, almonds, macadamia nuts, Brazilian nuts, cashews, pistachios, pine nuts, etc.

Pastas: soba noodles, rice noodles, egg-free pasta.

Dried fruit: dried apricots, raisins, cranberries, dates.

Sweeteners: maple syrup, agave syrup, applesauce, date syrup, pomegranate syrup, blackstrap molasses, tapioca.

Spices: salt, pepper, curry, paprika, cayenne pepper, turmeric, cumin, bay leaves, onion and garlic powder, garam masala, curry paste, etc.

Oils: extra-virgin olive oil, coconut oil, sesame oil, canola oil, and other vegetable oils.

Vinegars: apple cider vinegar, white and red wine vinegars, rice vinegar

Other canned goods: peeled tomatoes, tomato concentrate, chopped tomatoes, tomato sauce

Label reading Label reading is essential for a vegan. In the beginning, it may seem like a daunting task, but soon you will get familiar with the ingredients. The key is to go for products with short ingredient lists.

Foods that you must avoid: beef, poultry, pork, game, fowl, animal seafood, dairy, eggs, or any other animal-derived products.

Hidden animal-based Ingredients: albumen, beeswax, allantoin, blood, bone china, bone char, carmine, castoreum, casein, cochineal, emu oil, elastin, gelatine, isinglass, honey, keratin, lanolin, lactic acid, lard, retinol, rennet, shellac, tallow, squalene, yellow grease, whey.

Products to pay attention to: wine, beer, sugar

Ingredients that may be vegan: Allantoin, retinol, lactic acid, and squalene

Controversial Ingredients: silk, honey, insect products, or palm oil

Meat replacements: it is best to cook your own food than buy any processed foods. From an environmental perspective, processing damages the environment.

Chapter Two: Introduction to Foodi

The Foodi is the most versatile and easy to use kitchen appliance you will ever own. It's a slow cooker, electric pressure cooker, air fryer, sauté pan, a rice cooker all in one. The combination of pressure cooker and air fryer will cook your food faster and more efficiently than any other tool in your kitchen. You can make all your favorite meals in the Foodi Cooker.

The Foodi Cooker is top-notch. You will be impressed with how well it cooks your favorite food. It works fast, it is easy to set up and use in the kitchen. Therefore, if you're new to using a multi-cooker, you'll get used to it quick and easy. You can use your multi-cooker manually or opt for some of seven preset programs. Programs. An easy-to-use interface allows you to easily select your desired cooking program.

Function Buttons in Foodi Cooker

Pressure
Release Valve
Easily release pressure.

Pressure Lid
Quickly tenderize and
cook ingredients.

Reversible Rack
Use to steam, or reverse
to broil.

Cook & Crisp
Basket
4-quart nonstick,
ceramic-coated basket
fits 3 lbs of French fries.

Crisping Lid
Use to finish off pressure
cooked recipes or to air fry
your food.

Cooking Pot
6.5-quart nonstick,
ceramic-coated cooking
pot fits a 6-lb roast

14 Levels of Safety
Passed rigorous testing to
earn UL safety certification,
giving you peace of mind.

PRESSURE COOK – this is the most common function of your Food Cooker. How does it work? Here are basic steps:

1. Lock the pressure lid and turn the valve to seal;

2. Set the time and adjust temperature;

3. Wait for unit to build pressure;

4. When cooking is complete, the unit will beep so you can release the pressure; otherwise, unit will switch to the KEEP WARM function. This is the common function because you can control the time and temperature yourself and customize them according to your recipe or your personal preferences.

STEAM – this is an ideal program for delicate foods such as vegetables and seafood because they require short cooking time, preheated steam and precise temperature control. You will be able to prepare fresh frozen foods in less than no time. For instance, beets can be completely steamed in about 15 minutes, cabbage in 3 minutes, and cauliflower will be cooked in 2 minutes. Use a reversible rack that comes with your device in lower position.

SLOW COOK – you can have your dinner ready for when you come back home. Use this program for slow cooking and simmering.

SAUTE/SEAR – go one step further and use this mode to brown meats, sauté vegetables, and thicken the sauces and gravies; cooking on this setting can maximize flavors, too.

AIR CRISP – you can "fry" your favorite food without drenching them in oil. How does it work? Use Cook & Crisp™ basket with this function. You can adjust the temperature between 300 degrees F to 400 degrees F according to your needs. Further, you can open the lid during cooking process to shake the cooking basket or toss ingredients with silicone tipped-tongs for even cooking; when done, put the cooking basket back into the pot and secure the crisping lid. Cooking will automatically resume after that. If you tend to fry smaller chunks that could fall through the rack, you can wrap them in a piece of foil. Use this function to reheat your meals, too.

BAKE/ROAST – this program works as a typical oven; you can make casseroles, frittatas, and desserts. You can choose a temperature between 250 degrees F and 400 degrees F.

BROIL – this program uses intense direct heat to cook food. It provides a caramelizing and charring that give your food that distinct flavor. You do not have to heat your grill or oven to achieve great results in the kitchen – just use a reversible rack in higher position.

DEHYDRATE – you can dehydrate your food in an easy way and have your own dried fruits and vegetables all year long. You can choose the temperature between 105 degrees F and 195 degrees F. Use the Cook & Crisp™ basket and a dehydrating rack.

START/STOP – Use this button to Start or Cancel a function or turn off your Multi-cooker. When you pressure-cooking time are up, it will automatically switch to Keep Warm.

KEEP WARM – once cooking is complete, the unit will automatically switch to this mode and start counting. It will take 12 hours. To keep your food safe, pay attention to food safety temperatures. To prevent your meal from drying out, just leave the lid closed.

TEMP ARROWS: Use the up and down TEMP arrows to adjust the cook temperature and/or pressure level.

TIME ARROWS: Use the up and down TIME arrows to adjust the cook time.

QUICK PRESSURE RELEASE – turn the pressure release valve to the VENT position to release pressure quickly.

NATURAL PRESSURE RELEASE – steam will release from the unit as it cools down. A natural pressure release can take up to 20 minutes, depending on the amount of food. When the pressure is fully released, the red float valve will drop down, so you can remove the lid.

STANDBY MODE: After 10 minutes with no interaction with the control panel, the unit will enter standby mode.

Advantages of Using Foodi Cooker

1. **Time-saving:** pressure cookers are time savers, and these features come in very handy for everyone, working-class parents, housewives, single parents, aging mothers etc. The Foodi Cooker has been manufactured with a great cooking speed that it becomes distinctive from every other kitchen appliance. The good news with pressure cookers is that as a cook, you get to spend less time in the kitchen, thereby having more time to achieve other things

2. **Safe and Easy to Operate**: As it is a very modern pressure cooker, you are reducing the risk associated with the stovetop pressure cooker. Stovetop pressure cookers do not always lock well, and you need to monitor the temperature and pressure gauges to make sure that everything is going well. Your Foodi Cooker self-regulates in terms of temperature and pressure, making it a safe pressure cooking option. Although you should never leave it on when you are out of the house, you can leave it cooking as you go about your business at home. Simply set it to slow cook and catch up on TV, do the housework. When you are done you will have a delicious meal from almost no effort!

3. **Preserving Nutritional Value**: Most of our existing cooking methods destroy or drain the nutrition of the food, and we are actually eating foods which are not able to fulfill the nutrition requirement of our body. Foodi Cooker Pressure cooking method prevents the ingredients from exposing to extreme heat. Pressure cooking also requires less time to cook, and so ingredients remain safe from nutrient destruction.

4. **Comfort ability:** The Foodi Cooker has a set of default setting with which a user could cook a specific type of meal without having to figure out the manual timing to set. For instance, the pressure cooker could help you cook your meat at a default setting and cook it fine.

5. **Energy Saver:** The lesser time you have to cook your meal; the more electricity you get to save. It is been established that the pressure cook saves 70 % more energy than any other cooking appliance on the surface of the earth. This does not only save your time; it also saves your money.

6. **Delicious cooking:** The fact that the pressure cooker cooks at an extremely high heat which is extremely higher than what is obtainable with other cooking appliances and this enables it to draw out more flavors from the food and thereby helping to preserve the taste by making it taste a lot much better than usual.

7. **Space, cost (and frustration) saving solution:** The Foodi Cooker can take the place of multiple kitchen tools, saving you space in the kitchen. Cooking at home seems so hard sometimes. Cleaning up is a nightmare for many homemakers worldwide. This smart appliance can make it all easier. Simply throw your ingredients into the inner pot, press the button, and go about your day. When you get back, it's like someone has been cooking for you and your family. You can use your Foodi Cooker in place of many appliances you already have such as a microwave, air fryer, slow cooker, steamer, warming pot, and rice cooker. You can finally declutter the kitchen countertops and cupboards with this nifty product! You will become more

organized, so you can efficiently handle every task in the kitchen. As for money saving tricks, the Foodi Cooker is a real magician! It can cook almost everything, from inexpensive meat, chicken wings and porridge to budget-friendly root vegetables and grains. Even leftovers are made to taste fantastic in your Foodi Cooker. The Foodi Cooker is energy-efficient as well.

8. **It is a great way to improve your health and lose weight**: The food you eat becomes the building blocks of the cells in your body. Opting for a healthy diet doesn't have to be complicated. The Foodi Cooker allows you to cook with natural foods, rather than using pre-packaged foods, so you can plan and stick to a healthy diet. You have a unique opportunity to fuel your body with vital life energy from high-quality food. Restaurant foods (at least most of them) are prepared using inexpensive ingredients, too much salt and sugar, as well as "bad" oils. Pre-packaged foods contain higher levels of artificial chemicals and flavor enhancers. By cooking your meals, you can control the type of ingredients you use; consequently, you can control your eating. Cooking at home is one of the best strategies you can do to prevent and control obesity. At home, you are in total control over the number of calories you're eating. The AIR CRIPS or BAKE/ROAST functions will give you the crisp texture and intensive flavor you crave, without consuming extra calories. The Foodi Cooker can help you lose weight in a healthy and natural way. Many studies have proven that people who eat meals at home are more likely to eat a variety of fresh fruits and vegetables, as well as consume fewer

sugary drinks. In addition, a child who is engaged in the cooking process at home is more likely to grow to be adult who has a healthy weight and good eating habits.

How to Use Foodi Cooker

1. Preparing your ingredients

Prepare ingredients according to the directions in the pressure-cooking recipe you have selected. For extra flavor, use the brown or sauté functions first, just like you would when cooking with conventional cookware. For instance, brown the meat and vegetables for a stew, before adding other liquids and cooking under pressure. Be sure to deglaze the pot, scraping up any browned bits clinging to the bottom with a small amount of wine, broth or even water, so they loosened, adding flavor to your food, as well as discouraging scorching.

2. Add Liquid

After the aromatics softened, add the remaining ingredients and pour liquid, into the cooker body, as specified in the recipe or timetable. This fluid is usually water. However, some recipes will call for other liquids, such as wine.

3. Lock the lid

Assemble the pressure lid by aligning the arrow on the front of the lid with the arrow on the front of the cooker base. Then turn the lid clockwise until it locks into place. Make sure the pressure release valve on the lid is in the SEAL position.

4. Select the function

Select the function, according to the recipe. Press the START/STOP button to begin. Your Foodi will begin to build pressure, indicated by the rotating lights. The unit will begin counting down when it is fully pressurized

5. Turn off the cooker and release the pressure.

When the countdown is finished, the Foodi will beep, automatically switch to the Keep Warm mode, and begin counting up. After the pressure-cooking time has finished, turn off the cooker by selecting "Start/Stop" button. You can release the pressure two ways: quick release and natural release, according to the recipe or timetable instructions.

6. Air Frying and Finish the dish

In some cases, after releasing pressure and carefully removing the lid, some dishes need Air fry, bake, roast, or broil to evenly crisp and caramelize meals to golden-brown perfection, finish with a crisp to create Crisp meals or simmer to help thicken, reduce, or concentrate the liquid; others require to add more ingredients to finish the recipe.

Cleaning & Maintenance of Your Foodi Cooker

Cleaning: Dishwasher & Hand-Washing

The unit should be cleaned thoroughly after every use.

1. Unplug the unit from the wall outlet before cleaning.

2. **NEVER** put the cooker base in the dishwasher or immerse it in water or any other liquid.

3. To clean the cooker base and the control panel, wipe them clean with a damp cloth.

4. The cooking pot, silicone ring, reversible rack, Cook & Crisp Basket, and detachable diffuser can be washed in the dishwasher.

5. The pressure lid, including the pressure release valve and anti-clog cap, can be washed with water and dish soap. **DO NOT** washes the pressure lid or any of its components in the dishwasher, and **DO NOT** take apart the pressure release valve or red float valve assembly.

6. To clean the crisping lid, wipe it down with a wet cloth or paper towel after the heat shield cools.

7. If food residue is stuck on the cooking pot, reversible rack, or Cook & Crisp Basket, fill the pot with water and allow soaking before cleaning. **DO NOT** use scouring pads. If scrubbing is necessary, use a non-abrasive cleanser or liquid dish soap with a nylon pad or brush.

8. Air-dry all parts after each use.

Removing & Reinstalling the Silicone Ring

To remove the silicone ring, pull it outward, section by section, from the silicone ring rack. The ring can be installed with either side facing up. To reinstall, press it down into the rack section by section. After use, remove any food debris from the silicone ring and anti-clog cap.

Keep the silicone ring clean to avoid odor.

Washing it in warm, soapy water or in the dishwasher can remove odor. However, it is normal for it to absorb the smell of certain acidic foods. It is recommended to have more than one silicone ring on hand.

NEVER pull out the silicone ring with excessive force, as that may deform it and the rack and affect the pressure-sealing function. A silicone ring with cracks, cuts, or other damage should be replaced immediately.

Useful Tips for Your Foodi Cooker

1. For consistent browning, make sure ingredients are arranged in an even layer on the bottom of the cooking pot with no overlapping. If ingredients are overlapping, make sure to shake half way through the set cook time.

2. **Watch out about overfilling.** Your Foodi Cooker should not be completely filled. Ever! You need space for pressure and/or steam to build up. Whether you are filling it with food or fluid, always make sure there is plenty of space from the top.

3. For smaller ingredients that could fall through the reversible rack, we recommend first wrapping them in a parchment paper or foil pouch.

4. **DO NOT** use a damaged removable cooking pot, silicone ring or lid Replace before using.

5. When switching from pressure cooking to using the crisping lid it is recommended to empty the pot of any remaining liquid for best crisping results.

6. Press and hold down the Time Up or Down arrows to move faster through the display to get to your desired time.

7. **Unplug from outlet when not in use and before cleaning**. Allow to cool before putting on or taking off parts.

8. Use the Keep Warm mode to keep food at a warm, food-safe temperature after cooking. To prevent food from drying out, we

recommend keeping the lid closed and using this function just before serving. To reheat food, use the Air Crisp function.

9. **DO NOT** touch hot surfaces. Appliance surfaces are hot during and after operation. To prevent burns or personal injury, ALWAYS use protective hot pads or insulated oven mitts and use available handles and knobs

10. To have your unit build pressure quicker, set it to SEAR/SAUTÉ HIGH. Once ready to pressure cook, press the PRESSURE button and continue as you normally would.

11. **NEVER** use **SLOW COOK** setting without food and liquids in the removable cooking pot.

12. **DO NOT** attempt to open the lid during or after pressure cooking until all internal pressure has been released through the pressure release valve and the unit has cooled slightly. If the lid will not turn to unlock, this indicates the appliance is still under pressure - DO NOT force lid open. Any pressure remaining can be hazardous. Let unit naturally release pressure or turn the Pressure Release Valve to the VENT position to release steam. Take care to avoid contact with the releasing steam to avoid burns or injury. When the steam is completely released, the red float valve will be in the lower position allowing the lid to be removed.

13. **Do not leave the house when it is on**. Unlike with a traditional slow cooker, the Foodi Cooker reaches high temperatures, can carry a high voltage, and involves literal pressure

Chapter Three: Recipe Conversion Table

Foodi Cooker Cook Settings

FUNCTION	Time	Temp
Air Crisp	1-60 minutes	300 to 400
Bake/Roast	1min to 4hr	250 to 400
Broil	1-30 minutes	Auto Set at 450. Not adjustable
Dehydrate	1hr to 12hr	105 to 195
Pressure	1min to 4hr	Lo
		Hi
Steam	10 20 30 min	No temp option
Slow Cook	6hr to 12hr	Lo
		Hi
Sear/Sauté	No time option	Lo
		LOMD
		MD
		MD Hi
		Hi

Foodi Air Crisp Conversion Chart

Type	Food	Crisping Temp	Crisping Lid Time, Fresh	Crisping Lid Time, Frozen	Oil?	Notes
VEGGIES						
	Frozen Hash Browns	350		20 min	Lightly Sprayed	
	Frozen Tater Tots	400		12 min		
	French Fries	400	20 min	400 @15-20 min	Spray	Soak 30 min prior if fresh cut
	Corn on the Cob	360	25 min			Foil Wrapped/Turn 1X
	Roasted Cauliflower	350	15 min		Rub with Oil	Add 1 cup water to bottom
	Green Beans	350	12 min			
	Tomatoes	370	10-12 min			
	Peppers	400	12 min			
	Roasted Asparagus	370	10 min			Preheat 2 min
	Whole Potato	370	35 min			
	Potato, 1/2 length	360	30 min			
	Red Potatoes	350	25 min			Shake a few times
	Potato Wedges	390	16 min		Spray	
	Baked Apples, Cored	360	20 min			Cut in half
BAKING						
	Air Fried Corn Chips	370	5 min		Lightly Sprayed	
	Canned Biscuits	330	6 min			Baking dish
	Frozen Biscuits	350		12 min		Baking dish
	Cake	300	25 min/Foil 10 more			Baking dish
	Quiche	360	20-22 min			Baking dish
	Muffins	390	15-18 min			Baking dish
	Sweet snacks	320	20 min			Baking dish

Foodi Air Crisp Conversion Chart

Food	Sauté	Time Fresh	Time Frozen	Pressure Level	Opening Method	Opening Time	Notes
Rice/Grain/Oats							
Basmati							1.5 cups water per 1 cup rice
Black Rice		20		High	Slow Normal	10	1.25 cups water per 1 cup rice
Brown Rice		25		High	Slow Normal	10	1.25 cups water per 1 cup rice
Grits		10		High	Quick Release		
Jasmine Rice		1		High	Slow Normal	10	1.25 cups water per 1 cup rice
Oats, Quick		1		High	Slow Normal	10	2 cups water per 1 cup oats
Oats, Rolled		10		High	Natural	20-30	2 cups water per 1 cup oats
Oats, Steel Cut		10		High	Slow Normal	10	3 cups water per 1 cup oats
Pasta		4		High	Normal	3	Cover with water
Quinoa		1		High	Natural	20-30	1.5 cups water per 1 cup quinoa
Risotto		5		High	Slow Normal	10	2 cups water

Wild Rice		20		High	Natural	20-30	1 cup water per 1 cup rice
White Rice		12					1 cup water per 1 cup rice
Veggies							
Asparagus		1		High	Normal	3	
Bell Pepper		4		High	Normal	3	
Black Eyed Peas		7		High	Natural	20-30	
Black Beans		26		High	Natural	20-30	Cover with water
Broccoli		5		High	Normal	3	
Cauliflower Florets		3		High	Normal	3	
Corn on Cob		4		High	Natural	3	
Green Beans		3		High	Normal	3	
Mushrooms		5		High	Normal	3	
Potatoes, baby small		6		High	Normal	3	
Potatoes, Sweet		10		High	Natural	20-30	1 cup water + rack
Potatoes, whole		13		High	Normal	3	1 cup water + rack
Pinto Beans		26		High	Natural	20-30	Cover with water
Veggie Chunks		3		High	Normal	3	1 cup water + rack

Chapter Four: 500 Vegan Foodi Recipes

Vegetable Soup

Serves: 10

Preparation Time: 35 minutes

Freestyle smart point 2

Ingredients

- 2 tsp sea salt
- 1/2 tsp black pepper
- 1 tsp basil dried leaves
- 1 tsp thyme dried leaves
- 1 tsp garlic powder
- 1 tsp onion powder
- 1 lb. carrots sliced
- 1 cup 15 bean mix dry
- 4 cups water
- 1/2 Tbsp minors vegetable base

- 1 cup onion diced
- 14.5 ounces fire roasted tomatoes
- 2 tsp sea salt
- 2 celery
- 12 ounces corn frozen
- 12 ounces peas frozen
- 12 ounces green beans frozen

Directions

1. Peel and slice carrots into 1/4" slices. Dice onion and celery t 1/2-1" dice. Rinse the beans
2. Combine all ingredients into the inner pot of the Foodi Cooke and stir.
3. Put on the pressure lid and make sure the valve is to sea Pressure cook on high for 30 minutes.
4. When the 30 minutes is up, allow to natural release for 3- minutes and then manually release the remaining pressure.
5. Serve and Enjoy!

Nutritional Information: Calories 175, Carbs 35g, Fiber 5 Protein 9g

Fresh Beet Greens

Serves: 4

Preparation: 13 minutes

Smart point: 3

Ingredients

- 2 bunches beet greens fresh
- 1/2 cup water
- 1/4 teaspoon black pepper fresh ground
- 1 garlic clove minced
- 1/2 teaspoon kosher salt

Directions

1. Trim the beet leaves from the beets. Cut the leaves and stems into about 2-inch pieces.
2. Wash the greens thoroughly. They can be very gritty and sandy.
3. Pour 1/2 cup water into the Foodi Cooker liner pot.
4. Place the greens in the pot and season with 1/2 teaspoon of kosher salt, 1/4 teaspoon fresh ground black pepper, and 1 minced garlic clove. Stir to distribute the seasonings.

5. Place the pressure-cooking lid in place and lock. Set to high pressure and cook for 3 minutes.

6. Quick release by carefully turning the pressure release control to vent.

7. Serve and enjoy!

Nutritional Information:Calories 2, Carbs 1g, Fats 1g, Protein 1g

Crispy Tofu

Serves: 4

Preparation Time: 60 minutes

Smart point 3

Ingredients

- 1 tsp. seasoned rice vinegar
- 2 tbsp. low sodium soy sauce
- 2 tsp. toasted sesame oil
- 1 block firm tofu, sliced into cubes
- 1 tbsp. potato starch
- Cooking spray

Directions

1. In a bowl, mix the vinegar, soy sauce, and sesame oil.
2. Marinate the tofu for 30 minutes. Coat the tofu with potato starch.
3. Spray the Foodi Cooker basket with oil. Seal the crisping lid.
4. Choose the air crisp setting. Cook at 370 degrees for 20 minutes, flipping halfway through.
5. You can serve with soy sauce and vinegar dipping sauce. Enjoy!

Nutritional Information:Calories 137, Carbs 24g, Fats 3.4g, Protein 2.3g

Crispy Cauliflower Bites

Serves: 4

Preparation Time: 12 minutes

Smart point: 3

Ingredients

- 3 garlic cloves, minced
- 1 tbsp. olive oil
- 1/2 tsp. salt
- 1/2 tsp. smoked paprika
- 4 cups cauliflower florets

Directions

1. Place in the ceramic pot the Foodi Cook and Crisp basket.
2. Place all ingredients in a bowl and toss to combine.
3. Place the seasoned cauliflower florets in the basket.
4. Close the crisping lid and press the Air Crisp button before pressing the START button.
5. Adjust the cooking time to 10 minutes.
6. Give the basket a shake while cooking for even cooking.
7. Serve and enjoy!

Nutritional Information:Calories 130, Carbs 7g, Fats 12.4g, Protein 4.3g

Curried lentil stuffed Peppers

Preparation Time: 40 mins

Serve: 4

Smart point: 2

Ingredients

- 4 Large Green Bell Peppers
- 1 Yellow Onion, diced
- 8 oz. Baby Bella or Cremini Mushrooms, diced
- 1 cup dry Lentil
- 1 cup dry Brown Rice
- 3 cups Vegetable Broth
- 1 ½ tbsp. Salt-Free Curry Powder
- 1 tsp Garlic Powder
- 2 tbsp. Fresh Ginger, minced
- 3/4 cup Raw Cashews, roughly chopped
- 3 tbsp. Tamari

Instructions

1. First, wash and prep your vegetables. Core the Bell Pepper and finely dice the tops. Add all of the ingredients to the pot of the Foodi Cooker, except for the Tamari, Cashews, and cored Peppers; stir well.

2. Close the Pressure lid on the Foodi, and set the pressure release valve to SEAL. Select PRESSURE and set to HIGH, then cook for 15 minutes; press START/STOP to begin.

3. When pressure cooking is complete, naturally release the pressure for 10 minutes, then quick release the remaining pressure by moving the valve to the VENT position. Carefully remove the lid once all of the pressure has released; add the Tamari and Cashews to the pot and stir well, but save some Cashews to top the Peppers with.

4. Equally stuff the mixture into the 4 cored Bell Peppers, and top with the remaining Cashews. Quickly rinse the pot out, place the Peppers in the Cook and Crisp Basket, and then place the basket in the pot.

5. Close the crisping lid of the Foodi and select BAKE/ROAST. Set the temperature to 360°F, and set the time to 15 minutes. Select START/STOP to begin.

6. Once cooking is complete, serve immediately. Store leftovers in the fridge for up to 7 days.

Everyday Use Veggie-Stock

Preparation Time: 100 minutes

Serves: 1 quart

Smart point: 1

Ingredients

- 1 onion, quartered

- 2 large carrots, peeled and cut into 1-inch pieces

- 1 tablespoon olive oil

- 12 ounces mushrooms, sliced

- ¼ teaspoon salt

- 3 and ½ cups water

Directions

1. Take cook and crisp basket out of the inner pot, close crisping lid and let it pre-heat for 3 minutes at 400 degrees F on Bake/Roast settings

2. While the pot heats up, add onion, carrot chunks in the Cook and Crisp basket and drizzle vegetable oil, toss well

3. Place basket back into the inner pot, close crisping lid and cook for 15 minutes at 400 degrees F on Bake/Roast mode

4. Make sure to shake the basket halfway through

5. Remove basket from pot and add onions, carrots, mushrooms water and season with salt

6. Lock pressure lid and seal the valves, cook on HIGH pressure for 60 minutes

7. Release the pressure naturally over 10 minutes

8. Line a colander with cheesecloth and place it over a large bowl, pour vegetables and stock into the colander

9. Strain the stock and discard veggies

10. Enjoy and use as needed!

Nutritional Information:Calories 45, Carbs 3g, Fats 4g, Protein 0g

Balsamic Broccoli

Preparation Time: 15 minutes

Serves: 4

Smart point: 3

Ingredients

- 1 broccoli head, florets separated

- 1 tablespoon olive oil

- 6 garlic cloves, minced

- 1 tablespoon balsamic vinegar

- Salt and black pepper to the taste

Directions

1.   In your Foodi's basket, mix all the broccoli with the rest of the ingredients, toss, and cook on Air Crisp mode at 390 degrees F for 10 minutes.

2.   Divide between plates and serve.

Nutritional Information:Calories 173, Carbs 9g, Fats 4g, Protein 6g

Brussels Sprouts

Serves: 4

Preparation Time: 5 minutes

Smart point: 2

Ingredients

- 1 lb. Brussels sprouts
- 1/4 cup pine nuts
- Salt and pepper to taste
- Olive oil
- 1 cup water

Directions

1. Pour the water into the Foodi. Set the steamer basket. Put the Brussels sprouts into the steamer basket.
2. Close and lock the lid. Press the Pressure button. Set the pressure to HIGH and set the time to 3 minutes.
3. When the timer beeps, turn the valve to Venting to quick release the pressure
4. Transfer the Brussels sprouts into a serving plate, season with olive oil, salt, pepper, and sprinkle with the pine nuts

Nutritional Information: Calories 137, Carbs 24g, Fats 3.4g Protein 2.3g

Roasted Vegetables with Tamarind Dip

Preparation Time: 10 minutes

Smart Point: 4

Serves: 6

Ingredients

- 1/4 cup balsamic vinegar
- 1 tsp black pepper
- Salt to taste
- 1 cup potatoes, cubed
- 1 cup green bell pepper, cubed
- 1 cup carrots, sliced
- 1 cup onion, quartered
- 1 cup cauliflower florets
- 1 cup broccoli florets 3
- /4 cup peas

For Dip

- 1/2 cup tamarind paste
- 1 clove garlic, minced
- 1/2 tsp black pepper

For Garnishing

- 1/4 cup sesame seeds

Directions

1. Mix all the dip ingredients to a bowl; set aside.
2. In a large mixing bowl, combine all the vegetables.
3. In another small mixing bowl, mix balsamic vinegar, black pepper and salt; mix until well combined.

4. Add the dressing into the vegetables, toss until they are well coated.
5. Preheat the foodi to air crisp mode, for 5 minutes.
6. Place the vegetables into the basket and bake/roast at 400F for 10 minutes.
7. When finished cooking, transfer the veggies to a serving dish.
8. Top with sesame seeds and serve with dip.

Nutritional Information: Calories 49, Carbs 10.52g, Fats 0.18g, Protein 1.59g

Homemade Carrot &Turmeric Soup

Preparation time: 55 mins

Servings: 2

Smart Point: 5

Ingredients

- 1 tbsp. olive oil
- 1 medium-sized onion, chopped
- 2 garlic cloves
- 1/4 tsp turmeric powder
- 500g carrots, peeled and chopped
- 1.2l vegetable stock
- Handful fresh coriander
- Salt & pepper, to taste

Instructions

1. Set your Foodi Cooker to Sauté mode on MEDIUM settings add
   1 tbsp. olive oil, add the chopped onion, crushed garlic, then
   Sauté until softened.

2. Stir in the turmeric powder and the chopped carrots – add the vegetable stock along with salt and pepper to taste, bring it to a boil then reduce the temperature.

3. Cover and Slow cook for approximately 30 minutes until the carrots are tender.

4. Put to one side and allow to cool to room temperature.

5. Pour the ingredients into the jug of your Ninja Kitchen blender, add fresh coriander and blitz until smooth – adjust seasoning if needed.

6. Pour back into a pan and heat through until warm.

Coconut, Peanut Butter & Chocolate Bites

Preparation Time: 20 mins

Servings: 8

Smart point: 2

Ingredients

- For the Peanut Butter Base
- 100g oats
- 1 tsp cinnamon
- 3 tbsp. peanut butter
- 4 tbsp. maple syrup
- 2 tbsp. coconut oil, melted

For the Coconut Filling

- 3 tbsp. coconut oil
- 3 tbsp. maple syrup
- 70g desiccated coconut

For the Chocolate Topping

- 3 tbsp. coconut oil

- 3 tbsp. maple syrup
- 5 tbsp. cacao powder
- Cacao nibs and coconut chips to decorate

Instructions

1. Place all of the ingredients for the base into your Ninja Kitchen Nutri Ninja blender and pulse quite a few times until the mixture comes together in a slightly sticky flapjack mixture.

2. Press into the base of a lined 15cm x 20cm tin or tub with your hands evenly. Set aside.

3. Next, melt the coconut oil and whisk in the maple syrup and coconut to form a slightly thick but spreadable mixture. Spoon this over the base to cover and use the back of a spoon to spread and pat down. Chill while you make the topping.

4. Melt the coconut oil then whisk in the maple syrup and cacao powder to form a smooth chocolate sauce. Pour this over the coconut layer to cover. Sprinkle over the cacao nibs and coconut then place in the fridge for at least 2 hours to set.

Remove from the tub or tin and onto a chopping board. Cut into 8-10 pieces and enjoy!

Green Lasagna Soup

Preparation Time: 30 minutes

Serves: 4

Smart Point: 6

Ingredients

- ½ pound broccoli; chopped
- 3 lasagna noodles
- 1 carrot; chopped
- 2 garlic cloves minced
- 1 cup tomato paste
- 1 cup tomatoes; chopped
- ¼ cup dried green lentils
- 2 cups vegetable broth
- 1 cup leeks; chopped
- 1 teaspoon olive oil
- 2 teaspoon Italian seasoning
- salt to taste

Directions

1. Warm oil on Sear/Sauté. Add garlic and leeks and cook for 2 minutes until soft; add tomato paste, carrot, Italian seasoning, broccoli, tomatoes, lentils, and salt. Stir in vegetable broth and lasagna pieces.
2. Seal the pressure lid, choose Pressure, set to High, and set the timer to 3 minutes. Press Start.
3. Release pressure naturally for 10 minutes, then release the remaining pressure quickly. Divide soup into serving bowls and serve.

Nutritional Information:Calories 253.5, Carbs 22.8g, Fats 6.5g, Protein 24g

Steamed Broccoli and Carrots with Lemon

Preparation Time: 10 minutes

Serves: 3

Smart point: 3

Ingredients

- 1 cup broccoli florets
- 1/2 cup carrots, julienned
- 2 tbsp. lemon juice
- Salt and pepper, to taste

Directions

1. Place the Foodi Cooker Cook and Crisp reversible rack inside the ceramic pot.
2. Pour water into the pot. Toss everything in a mixing bowl and combine. Place the vegetables on the reversible rack.
3. Close the pressure lid and set the vent to SEAL.
4. Press the Steam button and adjust the cooking time to 10 minutes. Do a quick pressure release. Serve and enjoy!

Nutritional Information:Calories 35, Carbs 8.1g, Fats 0.3g, Protein 1.7g

Stewed Cabbage

Preparation Time: 40 minutes

Serves: 7

Smart point: 4

Ingredients

- 13 ounces cabbage
- 2 red bell pepper
- ¼ Chile pepper
- 1 cup tomato juice
- 1 tablespoon olive oil
- 1 teaspoon salt
- 1 teaspoon paprika
- 1 teaspoon basil
- ½ cup dill, chopped

Directions

1. Wash the cabbage and chop it into tiny pieces. Sprinkle the chopped cabbage with the salt, paprika, and basil and mix well using your hands.

2. Transfer the chopped cabbage in the pressure cooker. Add tomato juice, olive oil, and chopped dill. Chop the Chile pepper and red bell pepper.

3. Add the vegetables to the pressure cooker and mix well. Close the pressure cooker lid and cook the dish on" Pressure" mode for 30 minutes. When the dish is cooked, let it rest briefly and serve.

Nutritional Information:Calories 46, Carbs 6.6g, Fats 2.2g, Protein 1g

Chili with Cornbread Crumble

Preparation: 1 hour

Serves: 8

Smart point: 7

Ingredients

- 4 large carrots, chopped
- 5 stalks celery, chopped
- 3 medium russet potatoes, chopped
- 1½ cups cooked (1 15-ounce can rinse and drained) kidney beans
- 1½ cup cooked (1 15-ounce can rinse and drained) black beans
- 1 cup corn kernels
- 1 tablespoon tamari
- 1 tablespoon olive oil
- 1 medium onion, diced
- 3 cloves garlic, minced

- salt and black pepper to taste
- Cayenne powder (Optional), added to taste for spicy chili
- 1 batch Vegan Cornbread Mini Muffin batter
- 1 (28-ounce) can crushed tomatoes
- 1 cup vegetable broth
- 1-3 tbs chili powder, added to taste

Toppings

- fresh cilantro
- vegan sour cream

Directions

1. Preheat the oven to 375°. Grease a mini muffin tray.
2. Prepare the flax "egg' by stirring ground flaxseed in a small bow together with warm water. Allow it sit 10 minutes before using.
3. In a large bowl, whisk together the cornmeal, flour, bakin; powder and salt.
4. Stir together the coconut oil, nondairy milk, maple syrup, an apple cider vinegar in a small bowl.
5. Add the contents of the small bowl to the large and mi thoroughly. Fold in the corn kernels.
6. Spoon the batter into the mini muffin wells, until they are jus full. Bake until the tops are crisp and you're able to stick wooden toothpick in and it comes out clean, about 15 minutes.

Root Vegetable Soup & Roasted Chickpeas

Preparation Time: 50 mins

Servings: 4

Smart point: 2

Ingredients

- 1 tbsp. oil

- 1 onion

- 2 cloves of garlic

- 2 sticks of celery, chopped

- 2 tsp mixed herbs

- 1 tsp turmeric

- 3 carrots, sliced or chopped

- 2 sweet potatoes, peeled and chopped

- 600ml vegetable stock

- Salt & black pepper

- For the Roasted Chickpeas

- 1 x can chickpeas, drained well

- 1 tbsp. oil

- 2 tsp paprika

- Pinch of chili powder (optional)

- Salt & black pepper

Instructions

1. Select SEAR/SAUTE and set to HIGH on your Foodi Cooker. After 5 minutes add the oil, onion, garlic and celery and cook for 5 minutes, stirring occasionally.

2. Add the herbs, turmeric, carrots and sweet potatoes and continue cooking for another 5 minutes.

3. Pour in the stock and salt and pepper then place the pressure lid on top making sure it is in the SEAL position.

4. Select PRESSURE and set to HIGH and set timer for 20 minutes.

5. Meanwhile, mix everything together in a bowl for the chickpeas and bake in a preheated Foodi at 190 degrees C for 15 minutes to roast nicely.

Foodi Cooker Cabbage

Preparation: 22 minutes

Serves: 4

Smart point: 6

Ingredients

- 3/4 tsp Old Bay
- 1 tsp garlic salt
- olive oil spray
- 1 head cabbage cut into 4ths
- 1 c water

Directions

1. Rinse cabbage, cut off stem, and take outer leaves off. Discard.
2. Cut head into 4 equal parts and put into your Foodi Cooker air fryer basket.
3. Add cup of water to your inner pot, put basket inside pot. Set to high pressure for 1 minute, then do a quick release.
4. Remove lid and drain water.

5. Put basket with cabbage inside back into pot. Spray with olive oil spray and sprinkle with seasonings. Close air fryer lid.

6. Set to 400 degrees for 16 minutes (or until the outer leaves are as crispy as you'd like them).

7. Enjoy!

Nutritional Information:Calories 58, Carbs 13g, Fats 1g, Protein 3g

Vegan Chili

Preparation Time: 45 mins

Servings: 2

Smart point: 3

Ingredients

- 1/2 cup
- 2 medium potatoes
- olive oil
- garlic
- salt
- black pepper
- cayenne pepper

Instructions

1. 1/2 cup water in the pot, pierced two medium potatoes and cooked for 10 minutes at high pressure; used a quick release.
2. Brushed the potatoes with olive oil, garlic, salt, black pepper, and cayenne pepper; air crisped at 350°F for 10 minutes.

3. Bumped the temp up to 400°F and cooked for 15 minutes longer.

Buffalo Cauliflower Steak

Preparation Time: 45 mins

Servings: 2

Ingredients

- 1 head of cauliflower
- 1 cup of water
- 1 teaspoon olive oil
- 1 teaspoon lime chicken salt
- 2 cloves garlic, minced
- 2 teaspoons Franks Red-hot seasoning powder

Instructions

1. Put 1 head of cauliflower and 1/4-ish cup of water in your Food and cook on low pressure for 3 minutes, quick release.

2. While the cauliflower was under pressure, prepare 1/2 cup sauc in a measure cup (1 teaspoon olive oil, 1 teaspoon lime chicke salt, 2 cloves garlic, minced, 2 teaspoons Franks Red-hc seasoning powder, water).

3. After pressure is released, pour the buffalo sauce over the cauliflower. Air Crisp for 15 minutes at 390°F.

Breakfast Porridge with Barley and Strawberries

Preparation Time: 25 minutes

Serves: 8

Ingredients

- 2 cups pot barley, rinsed and drained
- 3 teaspoons vegetable oil
- 1/2 teaspoon kosher salt
- 6 cups water
- 2 cups fresh strawberries
- 1 cup cashews, chopped
- Juice of 1/2 fresh lime

Directions

1. Combine the barley, oil, salt, and water in the inner cooking pot.
2. Secure the pressure lid; press the PRESSURE button and cook for 15 minutes at High Pressure.
3. Once cooking is complete, use a natural release; remove the lid carefully.
4. Drain the barley and return it to the pot.
5. Add the remaining ingredients and stir to combine.
6. Secure the crisping lid and choose the AIR CRISP function.
7. Set the temperature to 380 degrees F and set the time to 9 minutes; press the START/STOP button.
8. To serve, divide prepared barley salad among individual bowls. Enjoy!

Nutritional Information:Calories 301, Carbs 14.4g, Fats 47.2g Protein 7.8g

Winter Rice Salad

Serves: 6

Preparation Time: 35 minutes

Serves: 6

Ingredients

- 2 cups wild rice, rinsed and drained
- 1-pound Acorn squash, cubed
- 1 tablespoon minced Chile pepper
- 1/2 cup carrots, chopped
- 1/2 cup parsnip, chopped
- 1 turnip, chopped
- 3 teaspoons olive oil
- 1 ½ teaspoons salt
- 6 cups water

For the Dressing

- 1/4 cup extra-virgin olive oil
- Freshly squeezed juice of 1/2 lemon
- Sea salt and freshly ground black pepper, to taste
- 1/2 teaspoon cayenne pepper

Directions

1. Add rice, salt and oil to the inner cooking pot. Pour in 4 cups of water. Secure the pressure lid; press the PRESSURE button and cook for 17 minutes at High Pressure.
2. Once cooking is complete, use a natural release; remove the lid carefully.
3. Place a reversible rack over rice. Place the squash, carrots, parsnip, Chile pepper and turnip on the rack.

4. Secure the crisping lid and choose the AIR CRISP function. Set the temperature to 390 degrees F and set the time to 14 minutes; press the START/STOP button.

5. Drizzle the dressing over your salad.

6. Serve well-chilled.

Nutritional Information:Calories 214, Carbs 29g, Fats 4g, Protein 10.3g

Tofu Rancheros with Veggies and Little Face Salsa

Preparations Time: 55 mins

Servings: 4

Ingredients

For the Spice Crusted Tofu:

- 1 - 20 oz container High Protein Tofu or Super Firm Tofu (or firm that's been pressed for at least 1 hour), cut into cubes
- 1 teaspoon ground cumin powder
- 1 teaspoon ground chili powder or less if you prefer mild foods
- 1/2 teaspoon smoked paprika
- 1/4 teaspoon salt or to taste

For the Salsa Beans:

- 1 15.5 ounce can organic black beans, drained (save liquid to make brownies or chocolate cookies)
- 1/4 cup Little Face Big Taste Jalapeno Cilantro Salsa or your fav mild salsa
- 1/8 to 1/4 teaspoon liquid smoke to suit your taste (or use 1/8 teaspoon smoked paprika)

- 1/8 teaspoon jalapeno powder (or chipotle or cayenne) powder
- 1/8 teaspoon cumin powder
- salt to taste

For the Veggie Topping:

- 1/3 cup grated carrot
- 1/3 cup grated zucchini
- 1/3 cup grated yellow squash
- 1/8 teaspoon salt
- pinch black pepper

For the Base:

- 4 large flour or gluten-free tortillas I used Ezekiel brand
- 1 cup shredded vegan cheese or make oil free with my cauliflower queso

Instructions

Make the Spice Crusted Tofu:

1. Toss the tofu cubes with the cumin, chili powder, smoked paprika, and salt.
2. Preheat your Foodi to 390° in the Air Crisp functions. Once it's hot, add the coated tofu to your air crisp basket.
3. Set the cooking time to 5 minutes and when the time is up shake or stir the tofu. Repeat for an additional 5 minutes.

Make the Salsa Beans:

- Mix all the ingredients together in a small bowl.

Prepare the Base:

1. Take 2 tortillas and put on a baking sheet while preheating the Bake/Roast to 350 degrees. Sprinkle (or spread) 1/4 cup vegan cheese on top of each tortilla. Put 1/4 of the salsa beans in the middle of the tortilla and bake for 15 minutes.
2. This will warm the beans and make the tortilla crunchy.
3. Once warm add on the Spiced Crusted Tofu, the shredded veggie topping, chopped tomatoes or other veggies you'd like to pile on like avocado or shredded lettuce.
4. Top it all off with a heaping spoonful of Little Face Salsa!

Vegan fried ravioli in the Foodi

Preparation Time: 22 mins

Servings: 4

Ingredients

- 1/2 cup panko bread crumbs
- 2 teaspoons nutritional yeast flakes
- 1 teaspoon dried basil
- 1 teaspoon dried oregano
- 1 teaspoon garlic powder
- Pinch salt & pepper
- 1/4 cup aquafaba liquid from can of chickpeas or other beans*
- 8 ounces frozen or thawed vegan ravioli
- Spritz cooking spray
- 1/2 cup marinara for dipping

Instructions

1. On a plate, combine panko bread crumbs, nutritional yeast flakes, dried basil, dried oregano, garlic powder, salt, and pepper.

2. Put aquafaba into a small separate bowl.

3. Dip ravioli into aquafaba, shake off excess liquid, and then dredge in bread crumb mixture. Make sure that the ravioli gets fully covered.

4. Move the ravioli into the air Crisp basket. Continue until all of the ravioli has been breaded. Be careful not to overlap the ravioli too much in the air crisp, so that they can brown evenly. (If necessary, air fry in batches.)

5. Spritz the ravioli with cooking spray.

6. Set Foodi to 390 degrees. Air Crisp for 6 minutes. Carefully flip each ravioli over. (Don't just shake the basket. If you do, you'll lose a lot of bread crumbs.) Cook for 2 more minutes.

7. Remove ravioli and serve with warm marinara for dipping.

Quinoa and Potato Salad

Serves: 6

Preparation Time: 25 minutes

Ingredients

- 1/4 cup white balsamic vinegar

- 1 tbsp. Dijon mustard

- 1 tsp. sweet paprika

- 1/2 tsp. ground black pepper

- 1/4 tsp. celery seeds

- 1/4 tsp. salt

- 1/4 cup olive oil

- 1 1/2 pounds tiny white potatoes, halved

- 1 cup blond (white) quinoa

- 1 medium shallot, minced

- 2 medium celery stalks, thinly sliced

- 1 large dill pickle, diced

Directions

1. Whisk the vinegar, mustard, paprika, pepper, celery seeds and salt in a large serving bowl until smooth.

2. Whisk in the olive oil in a thin, steady stream until the dressing is fairly creamy.

3. Place the potatoes and quinoa in the Foodi Cooker Multicooker; add enough cold tap water so that the ingredients are submerged by 3 inches (some of the quinoa may float).

4. Lock the lid on the Foodi Cooker Multicooker and then cook for 10 minutes. To get 10-minutes cook time, press "Pressure" button and use the Time Adjustment button to adjust the cook time to 10 minutes.

5. Use the quick-release method to bring the pot's pressure back to normal.

6. Unlock and open the pot. Close the crisping lid. Select BROIL, and set the time to 5 minutes. Select START/STOP to begin.

7. Cook until top has browned. Drain the contents of the pot into a colander lined with paper towels or into a fine-mesh sieve in the sink. Do not rinse.

8. Transfer the potatoes and quinoa to the large bowl with the dressing.   Add the shallot, celery, and pickle; toss gently and set aside for a minute or two to warm up the vegetables. Serve and enjoy!

Oil-Free Chips (Garlic Parm Flavor)

Prep Time: 45mins

Ingredients

- 2 Large Red Potatoes
- 2 tsp salt
- 4 garlic cloves crushed or minced
- 2 tbsp. homemade vegan parmesan

Instructions

1. Thinly slice the potatoes. I recommend using a mandolin (I use a 1.5mm blade.)
2. Place the sliced potatoes in a bowl and fill with water. Mix in teaspoons of salt. Let soak for 30 minutes.
3. Drain and rinse the potatoes. Pat dry.
4. Toss the potatoes with crushed garlic and vegan parmesan.
5. Layer half of the potato slices in the basket
6. In no more than 4 or so layers. Don't overload the basket or the chips won't cook evenly.

7. Fry at 170 degrees F for 20-25 minutes, or until dry to the touch and no longer flimsy. Stir and toss the basket every 5 minutes or so.
8. Bump the temperature up to 400 degrees Fahrenheit and fry for an additional 5 minutes or until the potatoes have become crunchy.
9. Remove from the Foodi and top with more vegan parm or salt.
10. Repeat for the other half of the potato slices.
11. Snack away!

Potato Wedges

Preparation Time: 40 minutes

Serves: 4

Ingredients

- 1 lb. potatoes, sliced into wedges
- 1 tsp. olive oil
- Salt and pepper, to taste
- 1/2 tsp. garlic powder

Directions

1. Coat the potatoes with oil. Season with salt, pepper and garlic powder
2. Add the potatoes in the Foodi Cooker basket. Cover with the crisping lid. Set it to air crisp.
3. Cook at 400 degrees F for 16 minutes, flipping halfway through.
4. You can serve with vegan cheese sauce. Enjoy!

Nutritional Information: Calories 179, Carbs 36.2g, Fats 2.6g Protein 2.8g

Oil-Free Chips (Garlic Parm Flavor)

Prep Time: 45 minutes

Ingredients

- 2 Large Red Potatoes
- 2 tsp salt
- 4 garlic cloves crushed or minced
- 2 tbsp. homemade vegan parmesan

Instructions

1. Thinly slice the potatoes. I recommend using a mandolin (I use a 1.5mm blade.)
2. Place the sliced potatoes in a bowl and fill with water. Mix in 2 teaspoons of salt. Let soak for 30 minutes.
3. Drain and rinse the potatoes. Pat dry.
4. Toss the potatoes with crushed garlic and vegan parmesan.
5. Layer half of the potato slices in the basket
6. In no more than 4 or so layers. Don't overload the basket or the chips won't cook evenly.

7. Fry at 170 degrees F for 20-25 minutes, or until dry to the touch and no longer flimsy. Stir and toss the basket every 5 minutes or so.

8. Bump the temperature up to 400 degrees Fahrenheit and fry for an additional 5 minutes or until the potatoes have become crunchy.

9. Remove from the Foodi and top with more vegan parm or salt.

10. Repeat for the other half of the potato slices.

11. Snack away!

Crispy Tofu Nuggets

Preparation Time: 35 mins

Servings: 4

Ingredients

- 1 x 400g block firm tofu
- 1/3 cup oat milk
- 3 tbsp. almond flour
- 2 tbsp. plain white gluten-free flour
- 1 tbsp. nutritional yeast
- 1 tsp vegetable stock powder
- 1/4 tsp paprika
- 1/8 tsp garlic granules
- 1/8 tsp turmeric powder

Instructions

1. Drain the tofu and press in a tofu press to remove more water for crispier tofu. Use a tofu press. Alternatively, wrap the tofu in a clean kitchen towel and place it between two chopping boards, then pile several heavy books on top and leave it for 2-3 hours.

2. Once the tofu has been drained/ pressed, use your hands to break it into 'nugget' sized chunks. You can cut it into pieces if you would prefer, but I think the ragged edges are better to hold the coating and make them look like typical chicken nuggets.

3. Pour the oat milk into a shallow bowl.

4. In a separate shallow bowl, mix together all of the remaining ingredients.

5. Take a piece of tofu and coat it in milk, followed by the coating. Make sure that all of the sides are covered. Then place it in the Foodi Cooker Cook & Crisp Basket. Repeat until all of the tofu is coated.

6. Seal the lid of the Foodi. Select 'Air Crisp' at 400F for 20 minutes. Then press Start.

7. Once the nuggets are ready you can serve them with chips and beans or a side salad.

Baked Bananas

Serves: 4

Preparation Time: 12 minutes

Ingredients

- 4 firm bananas, peeled and halved

- 1/4 cup maple syrup

- 1 tbsp. ground cinnamon

- 1-piece fresh ginger, grated

- 1 1/2 tsp. nutmeg

Directions

1. Place in the ceramic pot the Foodi Cook and Crisp reversible rack.

2. In a bowl, season the bananas with maple syrup, ground cinnamon, ginger, and nutmeg. Place the bananas on the rack.

3. Close the crisping lid and press the Bake/Roast button before pressing the START button.

4. Adjust the cooking time to 10 minutes.

5. Serve and enjoy!

Nutritional Information:Calories 183, Carbs 42.2g, Fats 0.9g, Protein 1.4g

Peanut Butter and Jam Brownies

Prep: 20 mins/Cook: 40 mins
Servings: 9

Ingredients

- 250g oats (use gluten free if required)
- 70g cacao powder
- 1 tsp baking powder
- 1/4 tsp salt
- 75ml maple syrup
- 90ml non-dairy milk (I use unsweetened oat milk)
- 60ml apple sauce
- 50ml coconut oil (melted)
- 1 tsp vanilla extract
- 50g dairy free dark chocolate chunks
- 100g smooth peanut butter plus 1 tbsp. coconut oil (combined and melted in microwave for 45 seconds)
- Strawberry jam (use store bought or homemade chia seed jam seed recipe as follows)
- 200g strawberries (cut into small chunks)
- 1 tbsp. chia seeds

- 3 tbsp. maple syrup

Instructions

1. Preheat Foodi to 350°F and grease a square tin (or an 8-inch baking pan). with some coconut oil.

2. In your food processor, blitz your oats into a fine flour.

3. Next add cocoa powder, baking powder, salt and blitz again.

4. Pour in maple syrup, non-dairy milk, apple sauce, coconut oil and vanilla extract. Blitz again until combined.

5. Gently fold the chocolate chunks into the mixture.

6. Empty mixture into tin, before covering completely with the melted peanut butter.

7. If you are making your own jam, combine the strawberries and maple syrup in a saucepan on a medium heat. Let simmer for 5 minutes before, mashing into a jam like consistency and stirring in chia seeds. Let simmer for a further 5 minutes.

8. Add dollops of jam onto the peanut butter and using a knife draw swirls to create a marble effect.

9. Place into Foodi for 40 minutes, before taking out and leaving to cool for 30 minutes.

10. Cut into squares and enjoy

Sweet Potato Wedges &Smoked Paprika Hummus

Preparation time: 50 mins

Servings: 4

Ingredients

- 2-3 large sweet potatoes, cut into wedges
- 2 tbsp. oil
- 2 tsp paprika
- 2 tsp mixed herbs
- Black pepper & salt

For the Hummus

- 1 x can chickpeas, drained and rinsed
- 1 clove of garlic
- Juice of 2 lemons
- 2 spring onions
- 2 tsp smoked paprika
- 2 tsp cumin
- 2 tbsp. oil

Instructions

1. Mix together the sweet potato wedges with the other ingredients in a bowl to coat well.

2. Place the potatoes into the Cook & Crisp basket. Close the lid on your Foodi Cooker and select AIR CRISP to 200 degrees C and set time to 30 minutes. Check after 15 minutes to see how they are getting on.

3. Meanwhile, place the hummus ingredients into your Ninja Kitchen chopper and pulse until you have a smooth dip. Chill until needed.

4. Once the potatoes are soft and crisp on the outside, serve with the hummus to dip into and enjoy!

Sweet Sriracha Carrots

Serves: 4

Preparation Time: 27 minutes

Ingredients

- 2 tablespoons sriracha
- 1 cup water
- 1 teaspoon sugar
- 2 tablespoons olive oil
- ½ cup dill
- 1-pound carrots
- 1 teaspoon oregano

Directions

1. Wash the carrots, peel them, and slice them. Set the pressure cooker to" Sauté" mode.

2. Pour the olive oil into the pressure cooker and add the sliced carrots. Sprinkle the vegetables with the oregano and dill.

3. Sauté the dish for 15 minutes, stirring frequently. Sprinkle the carrot with the sugar, water, and sriracha. Mix well.

4. Close the pressure cooker lid and cook the dish on" Pressure mode for 2 minutes. When the cooking time ends, release the remaining pressure and open the pressure cooker lid.

5. Transfer the carrots to a serving plate.

Nutritional Information:Calories 103, Carbs 10.2g, Fats 7g Protein 1g

Vegan Mushroom Bourguignon

Preparation Time: 3hrs 10 mins

Servings: 4

Ingredients

- 250g white mushrooms
- 250g chestnut mushrooms
- 150g carrots
- 1 medium onion
- 3 cloves of garlic
- 1 tsp dried oregano
- 2 bay leaves
- 400ml vegetable stock
- 500ml vegan red wine
- 1 tbsp. tomato paste
- 2 tbsp. fresh thyme
- 2 tbsp. olive oil
- Salt and pepper to taste
- 3 tbsp. whole wheat flour

Instructions

1. Begin by preparing the vegetables, washing the mushrooms and carrots.

2. Slice the mushrooms into thick slices, dice the carrots into approx.2cm chunks, thinly slice the onion and crush the garlic.

3. Place all of the ingredients into the pot of your FOODI COOKER and mix to combine well.

4. Place the lid over the pot of the FOODI COOKER; select SLOW COOK on HI and cook for 2-3 hours.

5. Serve whilst warm and store the remaining in the fridge.

Vegan Chili

Preparation Time: 45 mins

Servings: 2

Ingredients

- 1/2 cup
- 2 medium potatoes
- olive oil
- garlic
- salt
- black pepper
- cayenne pepper

Instructions

4. 1/2 cup water in the pot, pierced two medium potatoes and cooked for 10 minutes at high pressure; used a quick release.

5. Brushed the potatoes with olive oil, garlic, salt, black pepper, and cayenne pepper; air crisped at 350°F for 10 minutes.

6. Bumped the temp up to 400°F and cooked for 15 minutes longer.

Potato Wedges

Serves: 4

Preparation Time: 40 minutes

Ingredients

- 1 lb. potatoes, sliced into wedges
- 1 tsp. olive oil
- Salt and pepper, to taste
- 1/2 tsp. garlic powder

Directions

5. Coat the potatoes with oil. Season with salt, pepper and garlic powder
6. Add the potatoes in the Foodi Cooker basket. Cover with the crisping lid. Set it to air crisp.
7. Cook at 400 degrees F for 16 minutes, flipping halfway through.
8. You can serve with vegan cheese sauce. Enjoy!

Nutritional Information:Calories 179, Carbs 36.2g, Fats 2.6g, Protein 2.8g

Foodi Cooker Steak Fries

Serves: 4

Preparation Time: 25 minutes

Ingredients

- 4 Russet Potatoes
- 1 tbsp slap yo mama (optional)
- 1 cup water
- 1/2 cup olive oil

Directions

1. Cut your potatoes into 1/2-inch wedges
2. Mix together Slap yo mama spices and olive oil
3. If you don't like the spicy seasonings you can use paprika, and garlic powder, salt pepper mixed with your olive oil.
4. Coat your fries with the seasonings
5. Place one cup water in the bottom of your foodi. Place fries in your air fryer basket
6. cook on high pressure for 10 minutes. Do a quick release
7. Remove the pressure cooker lid

8. Place on air crisp 400 degrees for 10 minutes. Open after 5 minutes to stir.

Roasted Vegetables with Tamarind Dip

Serves: 6

Preparation: 10 mins

Ingredients

- 1 cup potatoes, cubed
- 1 cup green bell pepper, cubed
- 1 cup carrots, sliced
- 1 cup onion, quartered
- 1 cup cauliflower florets
- 1/4 cup balsamic vinegar
- 1 tsp black pepper
- Salt to taste
- 1 cup broccoli florets
- 3/4 cup peas

For Dip

- 1/2 cup tamarind paste
- 1 clove garlic, minced
- 1/2 tsp black pepper

For Garnishing

- 1/4 cup sesame seeds

Directions

1. Mix all the dip ingredients to a bowl; set aside.
2. In a large mixing bowl, combine all the vegetables.

3. In another small mixing bowl, mix balsamic vinegar, black pepper and salt; mix until well combined.

4. Add the dressing into the vegetables, toss until they are well coated.

5. Preheat the foodi to air crisp mode, for 5 minutes.

6. Place the vegetables into the basket and bake/roast at 400F for 10 minutes.

7. When finished cooking, transfer the veggies to a serving dish. 8. Top with sesame seeds and serve with dip.

Nutritional Information:Calories 49, Carbs 10.52g, Fats 0.18g, Protein 1.59g

Chocolate Orange & Almond Granola

Prep: 20 mins/Cook: 30 mins

Servings: 4

Ingredients

- 200g oats
- 60g almonds
- 3 tbsp. coconut oil (melted)
- 4 tbsp. Orange Blossom Vegan Honea
- 1 heaped tbsp. cacao powder
- 1 tsp cinnamon powder
- Zest of 1/2 orange
- Pinch of salt

Instructions

1. Pre-heat the Foodi to 325F.
2. Add the almonds to your Ninja Kitchen food processor and pulse for a few seconds until the almonds are broken down into small pieces.

3. Add the almond pieces to a mixing bowl along with the oats, cacao powder cinnamon and pinch of salt.

4. Add the melted coconut oil, vegan honea and orange zest to the bowl and mix everything together well.

5. Spread the mixture onto Ninja multi-purpose baking pan evenly

6. When unit is preheated, place pan on reversible rack, making sure rack is the lower position. Place rack with pan in pot. Close crisping lid.

7. Select BAKE/ROAST, and set time to 20 minutes. Select START/STOP to begin.

8. Once baked allow the granola to cool completely before tucking in or transferring to an air-tight container to consume within 2 weeks.

Steamed Broccoli and Carrots with Lemon

Preparation Time: 10 minutes

Serves: 3

Ingredients

- 1 cup broccoli florets
- 1/2 cup carrots, julienned
- 2 tbsp. lemon juice
- Salt and pepper, to taste

Directions

5. Place the Foodi Cooker Cook and Crisp reversible rack inside the ceramic pot.
6. Pour water into the pot. Toss everything in a mixing bowl and combine. Place the vegetables on the reversible rack.
7. Close the pressure lid and set the vent to SEAL.
8. Press the Steam button and adjust the cooking time to 10 minutes. Do a quick pressure release. Serve and enjoy!

Nutritional Information:Calories 35, Carbs 8.1g, Fats 0.3g, Protein 1.7g

Asparagus and Chives

Preparation Time: 17 minutes

Serves: 4

Ingredients

- 1-pound asparagus, trimmed
- 2 tablespoons balsamic vinegar
- Salt and black pepper to the taste
- 1 tablespoon olive oil
- 2 tablespoons chives, chopped

Directions

1.   Put the reversible rack in the Foodi, add the baking pan and mix all the ingredients inside.

2.   Cook on Baking mode at 390 degrees F for 12 minutes, divide everything between plates and serve.

Nutritional Information:Calories 174, Carbs 12g, Fats 6g Protein 7g

Crispy Cauliflower Bites

Preparation Time: 12 minutes

Serves: 4

Ingredients

- 3 garlic cloves, minced
- 1 tbsp. olive oil
- 1/2 tsp. salt
- 1/2 tsp. smoked paprika
- 4 cups cauliflower florets

Directions

8. Place in the ceramic pot the Foodi Cook and Crisp basket.
9. Place all ingredients in a bowl and toss to combine.
10. Place the seasoned cauliflower florets in the basket.
11. Close the crisping lid and press the Air Crisp button before pressing the START button.
12. Adjust the cooking time to 10 minutes.
13. Give the basket a shake while cooking for even cooking.
14. Serve and enjoy!

Nutritional Information: Calories 130, Carbs 7g, Fats 12.4g, Protein 4.3g

Cauliflower Stir Fry

Preparation Time: 40 minutes

Serves: 4

Ingredients

- 1 head cauliflower, sliced into florets
- 3/4 cup white onion, sliced
- 5 garlic cloves, minced
- 1 1/2 tsp. tamari
- 1 tbsp. rice vinegar
- 1/2 tsp. coconut sugar
- 1 tbsp. hot sauce

Directions

1. Put the cauliflower in the Foodi Cooker basket.
2. Seal the crisping lid.
3. Select the air crisp setting.
4. Cook at 350 degrees F for 10 minutes.
5. Add the onion, stir and cook for additional 10 minutes.
6. Add the garlic, and cook for 5 minutes. Mix the rest of the ingredients.
7. Pour over the cauliflower before serving.
8. You can garnish with chopped scallions. Enjoy!

Nutritional Information:Calories 93, Carbs 12g, Fats 3g, Protein 4g

Stewed Cabbage

Preparation Time: 40 minutes

Serves: 7

Ingredients

- 13 ounces cabbage
- 2 red bell pepper
- ¼ Chile pepper
- 1 cup tomato juice
- 1 tablespoon olive oil
- 1 teaspoon salt
- 1 teaspoon paprika
- 1 teaspoon basil
- ½ cup dill, chopped

Directions

4. Wash the cabbage and chop it into tiny pieces. Sprinkle the chopped cabbage with the salt, paprika, and basil and mix well using your hands.

5. Transfer the chopped cabbage in the pressure cooker. Add tomato juice, olive oil, and chopped dill. Chop the Chile pepper and red bell pepper.

6. Add the vegetables to the pressure cooker and mix well. Close the pressure cooker lid and cook the dish on" Pressure" mode for 30 minutes. When the dish is cooked, let it rest briefly and serve.

Nutritional Information: Calories 46, Carbs 6.6g, Fats 2.2g, Protein 1g

Teriyaki Glazed Aubergine

Prep: 40 mins

Servings: 8

Ingredients

- 1 large aubergine
- 1 tbsp. sesame oil
- 1 tbsp. tamari sauce
- 1 tbsp. agave syrup
- Pinch grated ginger
- 1 garlic clove - crushed
- Pinch chilli flakes
- 1/2 lime - juiced
- Sprinkle sesame seeds

Instructions

1. Slice the aubergine in half-length ways and score a Criss cross pattern over the inside of both pieces (this will help the marinade to absorb all the flavor)

2. Coat the aubergine in a tsp of sesame oil and rub this all over. Place the aubergine into the cooking basket with 150ml water in the bottom of the Foodi Cooker. Set to 'Air Crisp' at 375F and cook for 10 minutes.

3. Meanwhile, mix together the sesame oil, tamari, agave, ginger garlic, lime and chilli flakes to make the marinade. Add a splash of water if needed. You want the mixture to be a little sticky.

4. Pour this over the aubergine and into all of the slits you made earlier, then cook for a further 15 minutes until beautifully soft and crisp around the edges.

5. Sprinkle with sesame seeds and serve!

Baked Bananas

Serves: 4

Preparation Time: 12 minutes

Ingredients

- 4 firm bananas, peeled and halved

- 1/4 cup maple syrup

- 1 tbsp. ground cinnamon

- 1-piece fresh ginger, grated

- 1 1/2 tsp. nutmeg

Directions

6. Place in the ceramic pot the Foodi Cook and Crisp reversible rack.

7. In a bowl, season the bananas with maple syrup, ground cinnamon, ginger, and nutmeg. Place the bananas on the rack.

8. Close the crisping lid and press the Bake/Roast button before pressing the START button.

9. Adjust the cooking time to 10 minutes.

10. Serve and enjoy!

Nutritional Information:Calories 183, Carbs 42.2g, Fats 0.9g, Protein 1.4g

Asparagus and Chives

Preparation Time: 17 minutes

Serves: 4

Ingredients

- 1-pound asparagus, trimmed

- 2 tablespoons balsamic vinegar

- Salt and black pepper to the taste

- 1 tablespoon olive oil

- 2 tablespoons chives, chopped

Directions

1. Put the reversible rack in the Foodi, add the baking pan and mix all the ingredients inside.

2. Cook on Baking mode at 390 degrees F for 12 minutes, divide everything between plates and serve.

Nutritional Information:Calories 174, Carbs 12g, Fats 6g Protein 7g

Gluten Free Pasta with Pesto, Avocado and Coconut Yoghurt

Preparation Time:25 mins

Servings: 4

Ingredients

Pesto

- 1 bunch Basil Leaves (about 20 grams)

- 30g walnuts

- 1 ripe avocado

- 2 tbsp. lemon juice

- 2 tbsp. Vegan coconut yogurt (or dairy alternative)

- 3 garlic cloves

- 100ml olive oil

- Salt & pepper, to taste

- Pasta

- 200g gluten free pasta (I used soy bean)

Toppings

- Toasted mixed nuts

- Baby plum tomatoes

- 2 tbsp. nutritional yeast (optional)

Directions

1. Cook pasta according to packet instructions, drain and set aside.

2. Add all the ingredients for the pesto to the blender and blend until a thick paste form.

3. Add the pesto to the pasta in a large pot and mix to combine.

4. If the pesto is too thick, add a little water to it.

5. Season and Top with Toasted mixed nuts, baby plum tomatoes and nutritional yeast.

Butternut Squash & Red Onion Dahl

Preparation Time: 15 mins

Servings: 1

Ingredients

- 300g butternut squash (peeled, chopped and de-seeded)
- 100g red onion (peeled and chopped)
- 400g red lentils
- 200g sweetcorn
- 200g spinach
- 500ml water
- 2 tsp vegetable stock powder (or 1 small stock cube)
- 2 tsp medium curry powder
- 1 tsp ground cumin
- 1 tsp ground coriander
- 1/2 tsp paprika

Direction

1. Add all of the ingredients, apart from the sweetcorn and spinach, to the Foodi Cooker and stir.

2. Place the Pressure Lid on your Foodi Cooker. Select 'pressure' for 5-8 minutes. Choose 5 minutes for firmer lentils and 8 minutes for a fluffier dahl.

3. Once the dahl is cooked be sure to release the pressure before opening the lid.

4. Stir in the sweet corn and spinach, which will wilt and cook through with the heat of the dahl.

5. Leave it to cool slightly before serving.

6. Serve with brown rice, fresh coriander and a squeeze of lemon

Sticky Date & Ginger Flapjack

Preparation Time: 40 mins

Servings: 12

Ingredients

- 250g margarine

- 200ml maple syrup or date nectar

- 100g dates

- 50g coconut sugar

- 100ml orange juice

- 350g rolled oats

- 1 tsp ground ginger

- 1 tsp coconut oil

- 50g dark chocolate, broken up into pieces

Instructions

1. Set Foodi to Bake/Roast and Preheat the Foodi to 350 F

2. Grease and line an 8-inch baking pan.

3. Gently melt the margarine, maple syrup/date nectar and coconut sugar.

4. Place the dates in a pan with the orange juice and simmer for 5 minutes until softened. Allow to cool a little then place in your Ninja Kitchen Nutri Ninja blender along with the melted margarine mixture and blend to form a thick syrup mixture.

5. Place the oats and ginger in a bowl, add the date mixture and mix well until combined. Tip into the pan and press down evenly.

6. When unit is preheated, place pan on reversible rack, making sure rack is the lower position. Place rack with pan in pot. Close crisping lid. Select BAKE/ROAST, and set time to 20 minutes. Select START/STOP to begin.

7. Bake for 20 minutes until golden then leave to cool in the pan. After 10 minutes cut into 9-12 pieces but leave in the pan.

8. Gently melt the coconut oil and chocolate and drizzle over once cooled.

Buffalo Cauliflower Steak

Preparation Time: 45 mins

Servings: 2

Ingredients

- 1 head of cauliflower

- 1 cup of water

- 1 teaspoon olive oil

- 1 teaspoon lime chicken salt

- 2 cloves garlic, minced

- 2 teaspoons Franks RedHot seasoning powder

Instructions

4. Put 1 head of cauliflower and 1/4-ish cup of water in your Foodi and cook on low pressure for 3 minutes, quick release.

5. While the cauliflower was under pressure, prepare 1/2 cup sauce in a measure cup (1 teaspoon olive oil, 1 teaspoon lime chicken

salt, 2 cloves garlic, minced, 2 teaspoons Franks RedHot seasoning powder, water).

6. After pressure is released, pour the buffalo sauce over the cauliflower. Air Crisp for 15 minutes at 390°F.

Crispy Artichokes

Preparation Time: 20 minutes

Serves: 4

Ingredients

- 3 cups artichoke hearts

- 2 tablespoons olive oil

- A pinch of salt and black pepper

- 1 tablespoon lemon juice

Directions

1.   In your Foodi's basket mix the artichoke hearts with the rest of the ingredients and cook them on Air Crisp at 400 degrees F for 15 minutes.

2.   Divide between plates and serve.

Nutritional Information:Calories 184, Carbs 10g, Fats 5g, Protein 6g

Vegan Chili

Preparation Time: 45 mins

Servings: 2

Ingredients

- 1/2 cup
- 2 medium potatoes
- olive oil
- garlic
- salt
- black pepper
- cayenne pepper

Instructions

7. 1/2 cup water in the pot, pierced two medium potatoes an cooked for 10 minutes at high pressure; used a quick release.

8. Brushed the potatoes with olive oil, garlic, salt, black peppe and cayenne pepper; air crisped at 350°F for 10 minutes.

9. Bumped the temp up to 400°F and cooked for 15 minute longer.

Buffalo Cauliflower Steak

Prep: 45 mins

Servings: 2

Ingredients

- 1 head of cauliflower
- 1 cup of water
- 1 teaspoon olive oil
- 1 teaspoon lime chicken salt
- 2 cloves garlic, minced
- 2 teaspoons Franks RedHot seasoning powder

Instructions

7. Put 1 head of cauliflower and 1/4-ish cup of water in your Foodi and cook on low pressure for 3 minutes, quick release.

8. While the cauliflower was under pressure, prepare 1/2 cup sauce in a measure cup (1 teaspoon olive oil, 1 teaspoon lime chicken salt, 2 cloves garlic, minced, 2 teaspoons Franks RedHot seasoning powder, water).

9. After pressure is released, pour the buffalo sauce over the cauliflower. Air Crisp for 15 minutes at 390°F.

Vegan Carrot Gazpacho

Preparation Time: 2 hr. 30 minutes

Serves: 4

Ingredients

- 1-pound trimmed carrots

- 1-pound tomatoes; chopped

- 1 red onion; chopped

- 2 cloves garlic

- 1 cucumber, peeled and chopped

- 1/4 cup extra-virgin olive oil

- 1 pinch salt

- 2 tablespoon lemon juice

- 2 tablespoon white wine vinegar

- salt and freshly ground black pepper to taste

Directions

1. Add carrots, salt and enough water to the Foodi. Seal the pressure lid, choose Pressure, set to High, and set the timer to 20 minutes. Press Start. Once ready, do a quick release.

2. Set the beets to a bowl and place in the refrigerator to cool.

3. In a blender, add carrots, cucumber, red onion, pepper, garlic, olive oil, tomatoes, lemon juice, vinegar, and salt. Blend until

very smooth. Place gazpacho to a serving bowl, chill while covered for 2 hours.

Nutritional Information: Calories 88, Carbs 10.7g, Fats 4.7g, Protein 3.2`g

Green Lasagna Soup

Preparation Time: 30 minutes

Serves: 4

Ingredients

- ½ pound broccoli; chopped

- 3 lasagna noodles

- 1 carrot; chopped

- 2 garlic cloves minced

- 1 cup tomato paste

- 1 cup tomatoes; chopped

- ¼ cup dried green lentils

- 2 cups vegetable broth

- 1 cup leeks; chopped

- 1 teaspoon olive oil

- 2 teaspoon Italian seasoning

- salt to taste

Directions

4. Warm oil on Sear/Sauté. Add garlic and leeks and cook for 2 minutes until soft; add tomato paste, carrot, Italian seasoning, broccoli, tomatoes, lentils, and salt. Stir in vegetable broth and lasagna pieces.

5. Seal the pressure lid, choose Pressure, set to High, and set the timer to 3 minutes. Press Start.

6. Release pressure naturally for 10 minutes, then release the remaining pressure quickly. Divide soup into serving bowls and serve.

Nutritional Information: Calories 253.5, Carbs 22.8g, Fats 6.5g, Protein 24g

Vegetarian Shepherd's Pie

Preparation Time: 30 minutes

Serves: 7

Ingredients

- 2 white onions

- 1 carrot

- 10 ounces mashed potatoes

- 3 ounces celery stalk

- 1 tablespoon salt

- 1 teaspoon paprika

- 1 teaspoon curry

- 1 tablespoons tomato paste

- 3 tablespoons olive oil

- 1 teaspoon salt

Directions

1. Peel the carrot and grate it. Chop the celery stalk. Combine the vegetables together and mix well.

2. Put the vegetable mixture in the pressure cooker. Add the paprika, curry, tomato paste, olive oil, and salt. Mix well and stir well.

3. Cook at" Keep Warm" mode for 6 minutes, stirring frequently. Spread the vegetable mixture with the mashed potato and close the pressure cooker lid. Cook the dish on the" Pressure" mode for 10 minutes.

4. When the cooking time ends, release the pressure and open the pressure cooker lid.

5. Transfer the pie to a serving plate, cut into slices and serve.

Nutritional Information: Calories 104, Carbs 12g, Fats 6g, Protein 2g

Vegetarian Moroccan Red Lentil Soup or Stew

Preparation Time: 70 minutes

Serves: 1

Ingredients

- 2 Tbs. of olive oil

- 2 large onions

- 2 cloves of garlic

- 1 tsp fresh ginger

- 1 package of tempeh

- 2 tsp of ground coriander

- 1 tsp ground cumin

- 1 tsp ground turmeric

- ¼ tsp cinnamon

- salt to taste

- ½ tsp black pepper

- 7 cups of vegetable broth

- 1 can crushed tomatoes

- 1 jar of ethnic cottage Punjab spinach cooking sauce

- 2 cups dry red lentils

- juice of 1 lemon

- parsley and cilantro

Directions

1. Turn the Ninja to Stove Top High. Include the oil and sauté onions and garlic.

2. Include all flavors and tempeh. Blend well for 1 minute. Include soup and tomatoes.

3. Wash and deplete the lentils. Blend in the lentils, carrots, and kale.

4. Decrease the warmth to Stove Top Low for 60 minutes. Blend at times amid that time.

5. Rather than tomatoes this time; I utilized ethnic cabin Punjab spinach cooking sauce.

6. On the off chance that you include veggies it is increasingly similar to a stew and thicker.

7. You may need to include extra soup in the event that you include a lot of vegetables. Utilize your judgment.

Nutritional Information: Calories 574, Carbs 49.7g, Fats 19.3g, Protein 18.8g

Asian-Style Asparagus and Tofu Scramble

Preparation Time: 15 minutes

Serves: 2

Ingredients

- 1 tablespoon sesame oil

- 10 ounces soft silken tofu, drained and chopped

- 6 ounces asparagus

- 2 garlic cloves, finely minced

- 1 teaspoon fresh lemon juice

- 1 tablespoon soy sauce

- 1/2 teaspoon paprika

- 1/2 teaspoon coarse salt

- Freshly cracked mixed peppercorns, to taste

- 1/2 cup fresh basil, roughly chopped

Directions

1. Add 1 cup of water and a rack to the cooking pot. Place the asparagus on the rack.

2. Secure the pressure lid; press the STEAM button and cook for 2 minutes at High Pressure.

3. Once cooking is complete, use a quick release; remove the lid carefully.

4. Cut the cooked asparagus into pieces.

5. Stir in the other ingredients, except the basil leaves. Secure the crisping lid and choose the AIR CRISP function.

6. Set the temperature to 380 degrees F and set the time to 1C minutes; press the START/STOP button.

7. Serve warm garnished with fresh basil leaves. Bon appétit!

Nutritional Information:Calories 160, Carbs 8.5g, Fats 10.8g Protein 8.9g

Ratatouille

Preparation Time: 4 hours 40 mins

Serves: 1

Ingredients

- 2 Tbs. olive oil

- 3 cloves garlic

- 1 medium size onion

- 1 eggplant

- 2 zucchinis

- 2 red peppers

- 1 can diced tomatoes

- salt, pepper and a touch of oregano

- ¼ - cup of basil

Directions

1. Include garlic, peppers, eggplant, and zucchini to vessel.

2. Cook around 5-10 minutes until the point that somewhat delicate, yet at the same time somewhat fresh.

3. Include the tomatoes, and flavors.

4. Mix and Slow Cook Low for 4-4½ hours.

5. About ½ hour before done, when veggies are presently delicate, include the basil.

Nutritional Information:Calories 104.4, Carbs 15.1g, Fats 5g, Protein 2.4g

Cabbage Rolls

Serves: 1

Preparation Time: 1 hour

Ingredients

- 1 Whole cabbage

- 1½ cups wild rice

- 1 large carrot

- ½ onion

- 5 cloves garlic

- 2 cans tomato sauce

- 1 can tomato soup

- 4 cups vegetable stock

- salt and pepper

Directions

1. Add all fixings to the Ninja. Swing to Stove pinnacle High and warmth to the point of boiling.

2. Lessen warm temperature to Stove Top Low.

3. Cover and cook dinner for 40 - 50mins or till the point while rice is carried out and cabbage is delicate.

Nutritional Information: Calories 180.7, Carbs 22.2g, Fats 6.5g, Protein 8.1g

Conclusion

This book will help you achieve all your aim as a vegan and I will advise you to also recommend it for people you love. Enjoy!

Printed in Great Britain
by Amazon

56791078R00078